To. Jake . . . .
. . . .

D0984402

'TO A VERY SPECIAL'® AND 'TO-GIVE-AND-TO-KEEP'® ARE
REGISTERED TRADE MARKS OF EXLEY PUBLICATIONS LTD AND
EXLEY GIFTBOOKS.

OTHER MINI GIFTBOOKS IN THIS SERIES:
Welcome to the New Baby
To a very special Daughter
To a very special Grandmother
To a very special Grandpa
Happy Anniversary
To my very special Love
To a very special Mother
To a very special Son
To a very special Couple

To a very special Dad
To a very special Friend
To a very special Granddaughter
Wishing you Happiness
To my very special Husband
Merry Christmas
To a very special Sister
To my very special Wife

Published simultaneously in 1996 by Exley Giftbooks in the USA and
Exley Publications Ltd in Great Britain.

12 11 10 9 8 7 6 5 4 3

Copyright © Helen Exley 1996
The moral right of the author has been asserted.
ISBN 1-85015-694-8

A copy of the CIP data is available from the British Library on request.
Written by Pam Brown
Edited by Helen Exley
Illustrated by Juliette Clarke
Typeset by Delta, Watford
Printed and bound in Hungary

Exley Publications Ltd, 16 Chalk Hill, Watford, Herts WD1 4BN, UK.
Exley Publications LLC, 232 Madison Avenue, Suite 1206,
NY 10016, USA.

To a very special GRANDSON

Written by Pam Brown
Edited by Helen Exley
Illustrated by Juliette Clarke

It is very easy to get out of the way of
laughing as the years pass.
One settles for a smile – until
a grandson comes along – and one
learns to laugh again.

EXLEY
NEW YORK · WATFORD, UK

A NEW LIFE

You have turned our settled lives upside down.

You have flung open windows closed

against the cold.

You have let in blazing sunlight on

our gently shaded lives.

You have brought a shout of joy

into our ordered quietness.

You have given us back life and hope

and adventure.

…

You were the best of bonuses.

I <u>never</u> thought to be a grandparent – but here

you are. And I am very nearly young again.

My grandson was four months old. Scarcely arrived.
And yet his eyes explored my face and knew me
and he gave me a smile of joy so absolute it was
worth a lifetime's waiting.

...

Cold winds turn the last of the leaves and a thin
rain patters down.
It could have been a sad time, a time of loss.
But then you came – a promise of summers
still to come.

...

How nice to be hugged by a huge grandson – it
makes an overweight old lady feel slender again.

...

HAPPY DAYS

Grandmas and grandads sometimes feel old and
flabby and dull – but then the door crashes open
and a small boy hurtles in with a torrent of
extraordinary news. And how can gloom survive?

...

The sounds to lift a grandparent's heart
are the pounding of small feet up the
path and the hammering of small fists
on the door.

...

How <u>dull</u> life was before you came.

How much joy

is packed into a little boy.

...

One arrives – and there is a face at the window – a

small face that lights up in absolute astonishment

and delight.

It is the greatest joy.

It is the greatest gift.

Thank you for that.

...

There are many kinds of happiness.

Many kinds of love.

But nothing to surpass the delight of a little child

running into one's arms – their face alight with joy.

...

You are the gold at the end of our rainbow.

...

WHIRLWINDS AND CHAOS

Grandsons are always on the move. They ricochet
from walls and trees and furniture. They swirl
like dust-devils. They leap and plunge like fish.
They are a blur. They are noise made visible.
And sometimes, suddenly, and for the blinking of
an eye, they come to rest beside a grandma.
And engulf her in a hug.

…

Going for a walk with a grandson is like being an
ancient sailing ship being towed by an over
enthusiastic tugboat.

…

How can a day be dull when one has a grandson?

…

It is very hard sometimes to love a grandson with
the voice of a sergeant-major, the in-built destructive
abilities of an elephant, the love of dust inherent in
a buffalo, the appetite of a grizzly fattening itself
for winter. But you do. You do.

…

Grandsons take you on roller-coasters and bumper cars.
Grandsons help you up and over rocks. Grandsons assure
you that scuba diving is a doddle. Grandsons encourage
you up castle keeps, windmills and skyscrapers.
Grandsons give you a turn on their mountain bikes.
Grandsons take you to rock concerts. Grandsons give you
a spin in their first sports car. Grandsons sit with you on
walls when you go a funny green.

…

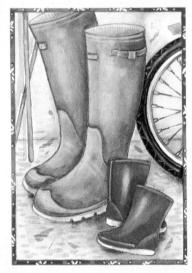

The phone rings,
"Grandma? Guess
what...?"
And then what
amazements follow....
...

<u>TOGETHER!</u>

No one can lose contact with the
contemporary world when they have a grandson
who comes visiting.

...

Grandsons are always greatly surprised to
discover that ancient grandparents know
quite a lot of useful stuff.

...

It's extraordinary what new interests
grandparents acquire in old age.
Rap and Soul and Salsa.
Bungy jumping. Snow surfing.
And, in turn, their grandsons gain new insights
into the way old gramophones used to play.
A liking for early Fords.
And a taste for newly-baked bread.

...

The greatest pleasure grandparents can have is for a
grandson to say:
"This book looks interesting – can I borrow it?"
or "Could you spare this for a little while?"
or "Can I have a turn at this?"
or "May I take a cutting from this rose?"
To share with you is joy.
Our lives link in the giving, in the taking.
In the smiles.

...

IT'S LOVE!

Never forget, not for a single moment, how
much we love you.

Wear our love lightly. Never let it be a burden. Let it
be an extra coverlet in the cold, dark days – and a
pleasant breeze about you when life is good.

…

We are such little creatures, you and I, yet we hold
in us mystery. For we are capable of love.
In the flicker of time that we exist, we will love
each other – and that love, my dear, can never be
lost. It reaches to the ends of all that is.

…

Grandsons are far too busy to come to the door to
see a grandma or grandad leave – for they are
Superman or Robin Hood or a creature from the
Black Lagoon.

But just before the car pulls out, or you set off
along the road, there is a hammering of feet
– and a shining face.

And a breathless "Luf you."

Which is the best of gifts to bear away.

…

There are no kisses as wet, as sticky and as heartfelt
as the kisses of a little grandchild.

…

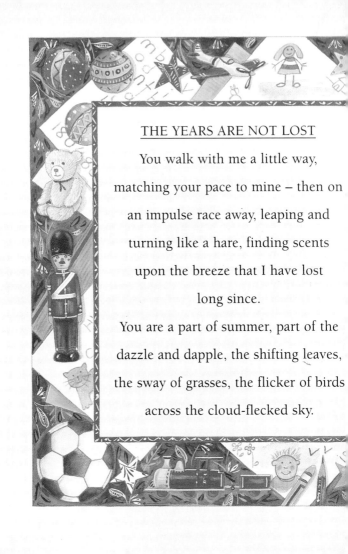

THE YEARS ARE NOT LOST

You walk with me a little way,
matching your pace to mine – then on
an impulse race away, leaping and
turning like a hare, finding scents
upon the breeze that I have lost
long since.

You are a part of summer, part of the
dazzle and dapple, the shifting leaves,
the sway of grasses, the flicker of birds
across the cloud-flecked sky.

And through you I remember how it was in the lost years – and share your laughter.

You circle back and take my hand. And talk as if you'd never left me. And I know, because of you, that however dark the world seems, however full of grief and loss, to live is the greatest privilege. To breathe the air, to walk in the sun – to hold a grandchild's hand.

TWO FRIENDS

You are my friend. You always have been – ever
since you took my finger when you were brand
new. Ever since you learned to smile.

We've shared a lot. First teeth. Scuffed knees.
Christmases. Birthdays. Long summer days and
winters by the fire. We've held sad services for little
mice – and wondered at the paws of newborn
kittens.

Mumps. I remember mumps. And the time that we
all got lost. And the time we ran and ran for the bus
and I puffed and puffed and you made them wait
for me.

Dear Grandson. I had begun to be old – but you
told me not to. So I'm trying very hard.

How neatly your hand fits into mine.

Wait till I get my keys – and we will go out and
find a new adventure.

...

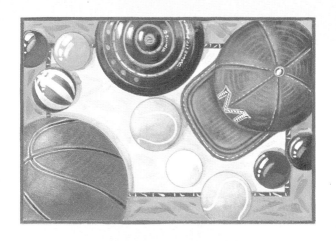

Grandparents and grandsons have a specially snug
place all of their own, where there are cuddles
and secrets and buttered scones.

...

Dear Lad. If ever you need a bolt-hole –
here's one waiting.

...

How good it is to feel your hand slip into mine –
and set off on a shared adventure.

...

<u>AGE? WHAT IS AGE?!</u>

Getting old comes as a surprise – for inside,
grandparents are still as young as they ever were.
So many people do not understand this simple fact
– but you are not bamboozled. You
look into our eyes and recognize us as
the same age as yourself.

A lot of people stop loving you when you get old
and lined and peppered with little
brown blotches. But grandsons like you that way.

...

It's strange to think you love as a grandparent
someone I scarcely recognize in the mirror. For you,
a grandparent has white-spattered hair, a double
chin, a comfortable shape; while I know myself to
be thirty, slim, dark-haired and agile. Still – by the
way you take me off to have adventures, I suspect
that somehow you know about the person who's
forced to wear this daft disguise.

...

Grandsons like to get on your knee and examine
your face, inch by wrinkled inch. The veins, the
wrinkles, the sneaky little whiskers fascinate them.
It's disconcerting. But who cares? They love you
exactly as you are.

...

JUST THE EXCUSE I NEED

Grandsons are the best excuse yet for playing with
mud, water and small steam engines.

...

A grandson like you is the perfect alibi to do all the
things old fuddy-duddies think undignified.
Who needs dignity!

...

Thank you for being my excuse to do all the things
I love to do.
With you, I can roll down sand-dunes, fly kites,
wade into ponds, skim stones, climb trees,
do the polka, eat lollipops and licorice bootlaces,
and read *Winnie the Pooh* and
Treasure Island once again.
Thank heavens for grandsons.
They give grandads a reason to play snap.
They give grandmas a reason to bake cakes.

...

Grandsons allow you to stand and watch
mechanical diggers, even in the rain.
Grandsons give you the chance to yell at football
games and eat sticky buns in teashops and talk to
bus drivers and try out computer games.
Grandsons make it all right to toast muffins over
bonfires in the garden.
Grandsons take one camping.
Grandsons share their toffees.

ALWAYS HERE FOR YOU

Grandmas and grandads exist to
listen and to keep secrets. And to
offer advice you can take or
ignore just as you wish.
With never a string attached.

…

If you're miserable or furious –
come round to see me. We can be
miserable and furious together.
Or talk it out.
Or just eat my currant cake.

…

Dear Lad. Never let disappointments or resentments or sadness gnaw away at your heart, believing no one else can understand.

Grandads and grandmas may seem infinitely old – but the memories of their childhood are as vivid to them as if those times were only yesterday. They have stood exactly where you stand.

If you need us, we are always here.

…

Here's a heart to love you, a mind to understand you, ears to listen and arms to hug. All at your disposal. Always.

…

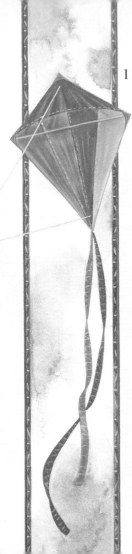

MY WISHES FOR YOU

I wish you happiness with all my heart. Laughter, smiles, love, hope, contentment. Joy in the ridiculous and the sublime. In little things and great. But most of all the happiness that comes from mastery of a skill. Which can outlast even love itself.

…

I wish you so much, but most of all I wish
you courage. Not battle-bravery, but the quiet
courage that endures, survives and never
loses hope. The courage that will sustain
you through every darkness, the courage that
will give strength to others. The courage that will
turn what seems defeat into victory.

...

I have such hopes for you – not fame or riches,
though they may come, but the enthusiasm to make
bold choices, to learn and experiment and make
and do. To weather storms. To learn from failure.
To discover goodness in other people.

...

I wish I could give you the lovely things lost in
modern tumult – the silences, the scents of summer
days, the velvet dark, the myriads of stars, the drift
of butterflies, the quiet streets.

...

<u>WITH ALL MY THANKS …</u>

Thank you for scooping me into your life – and
making me a part of your adventure.

…

One's children grow up and become sensible
and sophisticated – and, however loving, a little
weary with one's stories – and a little sarcastic
about one's singing voice.
But you ask for my stories and delight in my songs!
Bless you!

…

Thank you for all those squidgy kisses you gave me

once – and the pecks when you were growing.

And the snuggly ones you gave when I was sad.

You thought, no doubt, that kisses do not keep…

but, see, I have them all safe.

Treasures to see me through long

nights and dark days.

...

I want to thank you for showing me the things

I had forgotten; the complexities the

accustomed eye can miss.

Yellow-tipped stamen and furred leaf, the marvel of

a single feather, the glitter in a stone, the diamond

dazzle in a raindrop, the opal eyes of toads.

What can I give you in return?

Scones hot from the oven.

Cuddles on request.

My love forever.

...